In God's Hands

LIVING LIFE

IAN C KENSON

Copyright © Ian C Kenson.

All rights reserved. No part of this book may be reproduced in any form or by any electronic or mechanical means, including information storage and retrieval systems, without permission in writing from the publisher, except by reviewers, who may quote brief passages in a review.

ISBN: 978-1-63821-023-8 (Paperback Edition)
ISBN: 978-1-63821-024-5 (Hardcover Edition)
ISBN: 978-1-63821-022-1 (E-book Edition)

Book Ordering Information

Phone Number: 315 288-7939 ext. 1000 or 347-901-4920
Email: info@globalsummithouse.com
Global Summit House
www.globalsummithouse.com

Printed in the United States of America

CONTENTS

Introduction vii

Absolute Mearge Life, Living In Swampjungle 1
Initial Beginnings 3
Initialy Sara's Life 5
Local Movements Chaos 6
Menories Of Time 7
Watching Life EBB 9
Living Life Boost 10
Makaraba Fatality 12
Personal Death Loss 13
No Burial, No Cremation, Just Disposal 15
Life Bannishment 18
Saviour/Rescue 23
Makaraba Fatality 26
Canoeing Happyness 28
Tropical Storm Fishing 29
Rape 30
Rapist Arrested 32
Sara's Fears 33
Gathering Storm Clouds 34
Arrest Movement 35
Sara's Fatality 36
River Swamp Rescue 38
Sara's Lonely Battle 39
Swamp Water Reed Bed Rescues 40
Rescued Deliverance 41

Sara's Agonising Journey Home	42
Sara's Final Fairwell	43
Rapist Delivered	45
Honouring Sara's Life	46
Running Under The Tropical Storm	47
Prisoner Movement	49
Distruption Of Workers	50
Berritt Island	52
Conformation And Agreement	55
Fatality Compensation	56
Sara's Life Legacy	58
Prisoner Escape	59
As Time Moves On	61
River Rescue	63
Philomena & Barry	67
Acknowledgement	71
Frau Gertrude Shmitt	72
Payment Shortage	73
Recovered Payment Funds	75
Final Payment To The Makaraba Family	76
Escaped Prisoners Desparate Action	78
The White Man	82
Fau Gertrude Schmitt	83
A Women Scorned	84
About This Specific Book	87
About The Author	89

INTRODUCTION
UNDEFINED Life DIFFERENCES
Without Choice

When initially the thought of penning this dramatically sad living experience story, it was seriously considered, who would be remotely interested, obviously, it can be verbally stated and suggested to people who are by nature, considerate and caring, along with others who would require specific knowledge, because of their possible employment along with the area locations.

These vast and specific area,s, through out the tropical swamp area's of the world, of totally varying locations, that exist throughout the world, are by nature the exact opposite to the extreme desert area,s of the world, they have unlimited water in which millions of mangroves trees and bush's grow in abundance, thrusting their roots into the swampland ground, leaving little or no area,s of dry land on which people and populations can establish, or where they could possibly establish homes, houses or maybe buildings, allowing them to set up minor communities of populations, within these vast areas of swamps, other than utilizing meagre small clearances, where now these spaces are used as their living ground. These area's over the years are always under the threat of being taken over by the swamp its self, more and more mangrove trees and plants would sink their roots into the soft muddy swamp waterways, gradually encroaching onto the dry spits of land.

Therefore and because of these specific locations, where old and new growth mangroves re-establish their selves every year, families and people have populated certain places and area,s of slightly raised land area,s usually two to three feet above the high water levels at high tides, living their lives from birth to death, seldom if ever, never venturing beyond the swamp area limits, by the simple rule, lack of work and affordability.

ABSOLUTE MEARGE LIFE, LIVING IN SWAMPJUNGLE

Whilst having directly introduced members of the of public and communities of the greater world, to the absolute meagre living lives of these jungle peoples, in no way does it indicate or try to belittle them, simply because they were unfortunate enough to be born within these locations and be members of these communities that are forced by area and location to exist within these inhospitable vast swamp area's, nominally being residence of these jungle spaces, which are within the overall vastness of all swamp area's. Renders their life requirements, meagre to zero, to possibly evaluate this view point, a look or comparison to every day life living, has to be indicated.

Acknowledging every day sections of the worlds residents, become bothered about being respectfully dressed and presented, with their unblemished make up is in place and their hands perfectly painted, and undamaged as they flick them around, indicating their personal preferences.

Sara's daily choice is to use her hands to haul in her latest fishing catch, the skin on her small hands and fingers is stretched and torn, through constant use, never has she applied any soothing creams, she has always torn the skin cutting into the flesh, years of tears, along with fissures, have rendered her appendages as only useful to her jungle life and her hard work load, relentless every day she would be covered in mud, slime or any other substance the jungle vegetation would deposit on her as she passed or rubbed up against, bushes, trees, or the muddy extremities of the jungle swamp creek banks.

Because of their choice or by birth and needs, they live and function life through what ever the elements and nature throw at them, stoically obeying the rules that swamps and jungle affords them, their need for normality is that after darkness, it gets light, whilst after daylight, it gets dark, unless they live within the greater area's of populations, they have no powering source except naked oil lamps, also maybe a few battery torches, these have to be renewed as the batteries life always fades, consequently all life is put on hold until the daylight returns.

It is within this extreme dark night times, that the heightened fear times project their selves, applying these simple rules anywhere and everywhere within the jungle area's, anyone who exists at these locations, try to exist throughout the hours of darkness, without lighting or burning any commodity that involves a light source, as these sources of light reflect the fearful glow of hundreds of yellow eye's at water level, showing and indicating the huge numbers of crocodiles that frequent these swamps area's.

With the rest of the world living their lives by their area,s and locations, which usually are or can be upgraded and modernized, as their populations request or require, these unfortunately born peoples exist on meagre strips of uninhabitable jungle land space, that are always under attack from the ever invading mangrove tree roots, encroaching over the forever shrinking sections of dry land space, constantly subject to every element and conditions, that these locations would have to offer throughout their simple meagre lives.

INITIAL BEGINNINGS

The arrival into the swamp jungle located environment, that is hot, humid, extremely damp and wet, infested with insects, spiders, snakes, birds, animals and a very large colonies of crocodiles, is not the normal or usual location that springs to mind, consequently peoples and the vast majority of the worlds population, would not expect companies and governments, to extract oils and gas, from these specific area's, because they are huge treed area's, where every minuscule area of mud, in the water or out of the water, is rooted by mangrove tree roots, establishing their claim to any or all vacant land area's.

Arriving in Nigeria for the first time, the white man was excluded from the oil companies residences, simply due to miss information, finally being booked onto a cargo flight that would deliver him to the location designating as his area of operations, whilst the flight flew over vast area's of dense swamp jungle location area's, his initial thoughts were, anyone could get lost down there, never realizing how true that thought would be.

Chasing through numerous swamp area's, arriving at far and distant locations, it took him two days before being allocated a sleeping room, constantly on the move he and the other company engineer, slept on the launch these nights.

Arriving at the Odidi oil and gas process platform, a short time before Xmas, the company had released 90% of the work force that had spent 4 to 6 months within the confines of the jungle swamps, leaving only a skeleton crew to continue with the systems construction and commissioning

Overseen by directors from the companies head office, five in total, including one lady director, Dr Gurtrude Shmitt, they would spend the their time collecting and ordering equipment and required items, before the return of the operational staff, Xmas meal was served on board the staging platform, the white man had seated his self at the centre of the second table, the first being full, all five directors therefore had seated their selves around the white man, requesting to define what was needed to complete the platform systems, giving them a parts list, Dr Frau Shmitt, made a note in her diary, heavily under lining the name she written, one the of directors was dispatched immediately to Italy, to gather and collect these defined items, (over the Xmas period), returning four days later, before the new year.

With this gathered equipment now to hand, the revision on the valve systems progressed, but the systems were under sever strain, as the company was to enter into penalties on the 10th of January, @ 50,000$ per day, having 35 tests to carry out and complete, the white man devised and revised the test systems, cutting in down to only eight tests, in the next nine days, finally completing and signing off all tests, late on the ninth day, therefore informing the head office in Warri, all systems now completed.

INITIALY SARA'S LIFE

Mosquitoes had been vicious during the night, constantly dancing close to the scent of human sweat humidity had been very high. Scratch marks were etched on exposed skin.

Glancing over through the first light, it was clear that his condition had not gotten any better. Staring into the increasing day light, the surrounding jungle swamp began to emerge. Life had changed since the fair-skinned men had arrived. Every day large and small boats would speed up and down the creeks, washing swamp water over the dry stretches of higher ground, making the terrain wet with mud.

As the higher spit of land was barely thirty-five metre,s by seventy-five meres, there was little to no room for any buildings other than what the swamp and jungle provided. Always in abundance, homes had always been made of branches or heavy sticks pushed into the semi-dried muddy ground covered with broad, large leaves, usually banana leaves.

For more than thirty-five years Sara Umbilici, had kept the home going, badgering him when branches or wood had decayed or rotted, replacing the fractured leaves when the rain came in everywhere. Never in all that time had she ever spoken to him directly. She just indicated and pointed.

He would always paddled off to collect what she wanted, returning with what he had caught or collected, sometimes it was a medium-sized fish, sometimes a medium-sized snake, and sometimes a small crocodile. It was always something that would make up a meal. He always returned with the sticks and wood to repair their shelter.

LOCAL MOVEMENTS CHAOS

The boats from the oil companies that were building the stations throughout the swamps, cleared the main flowing watercourses, providing opportunities to catch fish farther away from the local village, canoeing, using these watercourses was sometimes extremely risky, as the main work over rig boats would cruise through these semi cleared channels, leaving very little room navigate around or pass, it became worse when these rig boats, spent days changing out specific sections of the well head mountings, they never stopped, always working at the well heads or racing up and down the restricted creeks, forever delivering or changing work over teams, through out their daily work routines.

The local jungle people would suffer because the constant activities around their area's would chase most of the fish away, scattering them out into area's that were not subject to this constant movement, impacting on the local jungle inhabitants, who would in order to catch enough fish, have to trawl into the outer creeks, they always avoided.

Not that this had any affect on Sara, she would regardless to these obstacles continue, to search for any types of food, that would made a meal, both she and the man she lived with, could eat staving off the hunger she felt when food was short.

MENORIES OF TIME

Her life was not made easier, as every day, when it was light enough in the swamp she had to prepare something for them to eat. This was mainly dependent on how many small fish, they had been managed to catch between them, or traded with others, who had caught more fish.

She had managed to keep the small fire burning, by placing small twigs over the embers, until the thicker wood caught if it was dry enough, fanning and blowing the embers into small flames, until flame readily shot up and ignited other sticks. Then she would hoist the cooking tin onto the bent stick over the fire and heat the swamp water laced with flaked fish. She them threw in some bark tree roots she had found in the swamp, which gave the cooked fish a tangy flavour.

She often sat staring at the swamp water flowing past the mud spit of land.

Many times she had heard machines above her head, noisy with engine sounds. Sometimes, more often than not, the dimness of the jungle swamp would lighten, making swamp trees easier to see.

The swamp waters often floated large water hyacinths, into the swamp's tangled mangrove roots, only to be washed out again when the swamp water drained with the turning of the tide. The only difference was spotting the snakes and baby crocodiles before they reached the spit of land. This usually happened when food was available.

Day after day had become month after month, then year after year. Throughout all of these times she had cared for the man who lived with her. Many suns and moons ago, she lived in a woodland village on the other side of the swamp, playing and running through the trees until she was been taken. She had seen the people who said their were her parents, taking paper money from the person she now lived with, at that time she had not known for why the man had given them paper money, only years later did she realize, she had been sold by her parents, for the reason they had nothing, selling her got them a little bit of money. She was taken away in a small canoe. They paddled through creeks, streams, and across rivers until they reached the muddy spit of land. She had been here since that time. How long? She did not know. Sunrise and sunset were her only ways of measuring time. Throughout the decades, not many local things had changed.

The sticky heat of the jungle swamp, mosquitoes, and insects that bite and leave sores eventually became unnoticed. The yearly time cycle was all that changed. The rainy season was always the worst. Thunderstorms and heavy rains lasted eighty-seven days, never leaving time to dry out. The daily heat increased as the sun moved across the equator, first northward, then southward. This year's storms had been more violet than any previously remembered. High destructive winds had raced through the swamps, leaving huge trees across the waterways. Movement became restrictive whilst trying to navigate through the shredded branches. The cyclonic winds had ripped timbers from the trunks of the jungle vegetation, blocking canoe and boat movements through the swamps. Fishing also stopped, making it difficult to find food.

As he was no longer able to paddle and catch fish, she was now the main provider, setting off at first sunlight. She would often return with only a few meagre fish that had dried out as she continued to search for better fishing areas.

WATCHING LIFE EBB

After she had caught something on her fishing trip, she would try to time her return as the waters from the main river flowed back into the recesses of the swamp, where the higher spits of land were. She would then moor alongside the hut she shared with him. The fire was, as usual, very low. Hardly any embers gave off any heat. She would slowly work on building the embers, as the flames caught the fine strips of sliced wood, she built the fire with more wood around it until a mass of flames rose up, the flames now held off the flies and other insects. She placed a tin filled with swamp water over the fire. She looked him over.

His breathing was short and raspy, making a gasping sound. He appeared no worse than when she had returned before. He gave a weak wave to acknowledge her. She had cooled the boiled water, which she gave him with the mashed-up fish and roots she had picked from a jungle tree. Exhausted, he lay back as she slowly washed his face with the remains of the boiled water. He made no movement. He appeared to be at rest.

She slowly climbed back into the canoe before paddling back into the swamp. Again she thought about what the other women had said. "If your man is not well, give him some of the hyacinth bulb roots, but only when they flower." She had not seen any yet as she paddled slowly into the main flow of the swamp.

LIVING LIFE BOOST

She caught a glimpse of the oil companies work boats. The white man moved his hand down, slowing the fast-moving boat. She was only two hundred meres from the land spit.

Her thoughts quickly turned to amazement as the white man's boat turned closer to the opposite side of the main flow. She could just make out a small naked child watching the boat as it passed. Even more astonishment look crossed her face as she saw small packages being thrown over the child's head.

She remembered there were other families across the main water flow. This pleased her, as she realized someone was thinking about the jungle-living families.

The child turned and screeched, joined by others, all of whom ran around picking up the packages. Everyone was now leaping, jumping, and shouting as they started to open the packages. Their voices were muffled by the sweets they had gobbled into the mouths.

She felt saddened because the other jungle families were being given something she had not tasted for many years. She slowly pulled on the canoe's paddle to continue her search for fish. Again her head snapped round as the white man's boat turned straight across the main water flow, heading towards the strip of land she had just left.

The canoe sped across the short distance she had just come, arriving just as the white man's boat neared the spit of land. He had watched as she had made the return, indicating for the local boatman to edge closer. He swung two small bags over and into the canoe. They landed in the middle of the canoe.

Nothing was lost.

She could see there was more than one thing in each bag. She shouted at the local boatman, who turned and spoke to the white man.

Turning, his smile said it all. He raised both arms above his head. He shimmied from side to side, clasping both hands as they were still above his head. He shook his hands. The meaning was obvious.

She copied his movement, beaming and laughing as she began to search through the thrown bags. Tonight, she thought when I spoon the mixture into his mouth, he would get something that would help him. Later as he opened his mouth. A faint smile touched his face. Edging backward, he tried to raise himself.

MAKARABA FATALITY

On that particular day, as she set out to paddle to the fishing area, there was many boats all going towards the Makaraba platforms, even at distance she could hear them shout and the roar of the boats engines, as they were racing in every direction. Loud voices would scream and shout as they raced backwards and forwards across the open water lake which bordered Makaraba platform area, which extend from the construction site platform, into the masses of swamp jungle vegetation, for the next three miles, over the next five hours, all of the boats and launches continued to race up and down, no one slowed down as they raced past the raised dry spit of muddy land, every one was looking at and into the masses of mangrove swamp tree roots.

PERSONAL DEATH LOSS

The effort to rise up was too great. He again sank backwards, laying flat on the piece of cloth she had laid him on. But he opened his mouth again.

The mixture she had made was laced with some of spices that had been in the bags. It was only a little amount, but it was enough to flavour the usual mixture she fed him.

Slowly he stopped opening his mouth, lightly shaking his head. She stopped feeding him. His eyes closed as he fell into a deep slumber. She lightly washed his face with a strip of cloth.

He never moved. Before she pulled the paddle out of the mud, she checked him again. His breathing was weak. His scrawny chest just about rose and fell.

He moved his head, opening one of his eyes. watched her as she paddled away before being swallowed up by the swamp vegetation.

He rolled onto his back. Gasping, he tried to fill his lungs with air. His chest rose as he again gulped for more air.

No more air entered his body as his chest slowly began to sink back down. Reaching the same level as the rest of his body, his chest never rose again.

All movement left his body as it seemed to flatten out on the piece of cloth. A last gurgling sound came from his half-open mouth. Flies and mosquitoes began to gather over his body, as if they knew he would not bother anymore to brush them away.

Throughout the old man's illness, the village chief had watched her struggle in her efforts to look after and feed the old man. He never once gave her any help, even when he choked, making it extremely difficult to breath.

He just idly watched, knowing soon he would pass away. Even as she had paddled away as the old man took his last breath, the village chief never moved. The jungle vegetation had swallowed her as she paddled the canoe into the swamp.

NO BURIAL, NO CREMATION, JUST DISPOSAL

The village chief motioned two of the women that lived with him, silently they moved across the short strip of higher ground, until they both stood at the lean to she had called her house, pulling the old mans body into the open air they stripped him of any ragged cloths. Leaving his naked body spread out, they arranged his arms and legs pointing out from his body, the village chief now stood over the body waving the bunch of twigs he carried, over each section of the naked body, turning over the naked body the women laid the old mans body into a section of muddy earth nearer to the swamp water edge. The village chief stopped his motions and threw the twigs onto the body, bringing his hand palm edge down onto the other hand.

Immediately the two women brought out the large cutting knives they had hidden in their cloths, slashing at the joints of his arms and legs, they hacked him into pieces, as each section separated they pulled it to the swamp waters edge, placing them slightly apart arranging them by size, each section slightly bigger than the last section until the complete body had been dismembered, only them had the older of the women taken one of the dismembered joints to the swamp edge and thrashed it around in the water, before placing it again amongst the other dismembered joints. Clapping his hands the village chief motioned them to return with him to the other side of the spit of land, sitting down and turning their backs on the grisly sight of the dismembered body.

After all of the previous years and the many dead villagers bodies, it still sicken him to carry out the disposing of the corpses, using the method he had accepted when he took over the running of the swamp village. Like his previous village chief had said, where, if we could, would we bury any bodies, there is not and never was any space or room to dig a grave, not in the middle of the second largest jungle in the world. Therefore it is always left to nature, within the jungle confinds there are vast numbers of creatures and animals that will instantly kill and swallow any unwary jungle dweller, human or animals.

The sections of the old mans body had therefore been left for the jungle creatures to cleanse the waste from the village, as had been repeatedly over the last eons of time, but it did not stop the tears that now ran down the faces of the chief and the two women villagers.

Dimness and darken came quickly to the jungle swamps, as little light would penetrate the dense vegetation, the village chief had ordered the ever burning fire to be stacked higher tonight with a large supply of extra logs, in order to increase the fire blaze as the darkness became blackness, only the shadows of the fire attenders seemed to move about, as they placed fresh logs onto the fire. With a suddenness the jungle noises dropped to total silence, then and only then could then could the frightened villages hear the slap of water, unseen the sound seem to come from many different directions at the same time, sometimes a more solid sound would be heard followed by a large smashing noise that made all of the frightened villagers shiver in fear, more noises could be heard with throaty grunting cut of with the sound of more water smashing sounds, the village chief ordered the fire to be piled higher knowing that the feeding frenzy would encourage the late comers to venture further onto the higher areas of the jungle dry land section.

Faint daylight could be made out through the over head branch of the jungle trees, for over nine hours the village fire had been stacked and re stacked, warding off the frenzy feeding of the jungle animals, mostly crocodiles, some had moved towards the cluster of the villagers huts, these were driven off by the villagers brandishing burning timbers, driving them back into the swamp water, smaller rodent creatures scavenged morals of flesh that had been torn from the larger portions, whilst insects in the billions descended over the blood laced earth mound, drawing up any last dregs of bloody moisture, attacking each other in there quest of being the final ones to be sated. Through these actions the humming buzzing sound of the insect mass terrified the village chief and the other villagers, for they knew there was no defence against the insects, should they venture away from the waters edge,

As the jungle released its darkness, the village chief moved slowly across the dry spit of high ground, watching for movement from any direction, wary that all of the feeding animals had finally left after gorging on the village waste that had been left, small pieces of flesh could still be seen, calling over the two women he stayed and watched as they cleared the dry land spit of the remnants from the frenzied feeding that had previously happened, sweeping every piece into the swamp waters, even then small baby crocodiles rushed in to devour the morsels, finally the village chief walked over to the old mans hut destroying every bit of the roughly built lean to, pulling out the four corner posts, the wooden framework collapsed, leaving a pile of aging wood, he signaled to the women, who moved forward with burning logs, throwing them onto the pile of aging wood, quickly flames burst through the heap, small animals and insects scurried away from the flames, finally the village chief indicated to the two women, who swept the still burning embers into the swamp waters, slowly they drifted away, the smoke trails curling down until the swamp water relinquished them.

LIFE BANNISHMENT

She had been gone for more than a week, staying over at swamp villages that were dotted through out the main swamp areas, every night she had thought how he was surviving, she reminded herself of all the other times she had been away, some how he had got through without her. She remembered the times when he had hacked his leg with an axe, he had survived then, so she continued to paddle the rotten wooden canoe along the edges of the swamp waters never venturing more then four feet from the banks, some times she saw half grown crocodiles scurrying away, she had traded some fresh crocodile meat she had caught, for other goods she needed, although she was no more than 8 miles from her swamp village, it was taking all her efforts to paddle against the incoming and out going tides that controlled the swamp water levels, finally she entered the swamp branch that took her towards Makaraba near her village, the tide was less here, so she put more effort into the paddle.

As she rounded the last bend before the village, her eyes sort out her home, her eyes caught the emptiness of the space she had lived in, a wailing scream erupted from her, echoing through the jungle branches, piercing through every branch and twig that made up the vegetation of the jungle. It seemed to hang on the very air its self, a second then a third scream rent the stillness that had descended in the swamp, nothing moved, even the insects and creatures appeared conscious of the tragic scream of despair, her eyes were still roving over every section of the swamp area, trying to find what could not be found, she could see it was not there, but she still did not believe it. She paddled closer to spit of land, edging the canoe directly at the point where her home had been,

The village chief stood from where he had been watching and waiting for the old women to return. He motioned her to move away, he stopped her from reaching the spit of land close to her former home, shouting at her whilst throwing sticks of wood at her, he drove her back into the swamp. Slowly she tried again, again she was stopped, the water inside the canoe was now covering her feet, she reached out her arms, begging the village chief to let her land. Shaking his head, he continued to hold her off, slowly she sank back sticking her paddle into the mud in the swamp water, quickly attaching a piece of cord to the paddle she tied it to the canoe, picking up small rusty tin she began to bail out the water from her canoe. The village chief spoke quietly to the two women both sat down watching the old women.

She had waited for the swamp to become totally black, before she slipped out of the canoe into the swamp water, what meagre food and cloths she had recovered from her lean to, whilst the village chief had nodded off, were now the only things in the canoe, as yet the swamp water only came just above her knees, but already tiny and small creatures were attacking her legs. Whilst millions of insects keep up the droning humming around her head and body, she had seen some small crocodiles begin to edge closer, splashing the water level with her paddle, moved them back, she rested her arms in a folded manor trying to find some rest, but these efforts were always interrupted by the creatures attacking her below the water surface,

Finally after the night time total darkness the dim daylight began to filter through, she found herself draped over her canoe, forcing herself upright, she clung onto the canoe side, picking through the food bits in the canoe, she swallowed some flakes of fish, daylight and movement brought out fresh attacks from creatures and insects.

With each tide change she noted that the swamp water rose above her mid waist, each tide brought fresh hazards to her, clutching onto the side of her canoe seemed to be the most sensible option. Tears began to run done her face, as she began to realized that what had happened so many times before to others, was now happening to her. She had seen other villages wives forced into the swamp waters, because their men folk had past away or had been knocked over the side of their canoes, only to be taken by any crocodiles that caught them in the swamp water before they could reach the swamp edges.

These other wives had been forced to stand in the water as she now had been. No matter how much they had cried or called out, no one had every gone to the village chief and had them brought back onto the spit of land. Unless they thought that the women had some use in them, meaning they might be young enough to maybe produce more young children or just to satisfy their own particular personal needs, condemning them to the fate the jungle held.

For over the past 40 years no one had ever survived the banishment treatment, the most had survived two or three days, before being missing on the forth. No marks or noise was ever heard during these banishment treatments, only the weeping and silent crying of the condemned women.

She had rescued a few meagre items from her now destroyed home, bitterly she thought home, what home, for more years than she could remember, the sticks he had pushed into the ground and covered with branch and leaves, had been her living home always depending on the seasons and the dense intense jungle surroundings, she or her man had never been beyond the only major African town she knew, Warri, where unless you had money nothing was available, only your-self, making the purchase of useful things impossible, stale food items were the usual things that could be bought, at a price, nothing was ever given unless paid for.

Forlorn she now stood waist deep off the edge of the dry spit of land, where the villagers lived, the village chief sat on his stool placed in the centre of the dry spit of land, he sat facing where the old woman stood in the swamp, never moving or speaking, he would order drinks and food from the other villagers by gesturing with his hand, constantly she pleaded with the village chief, he never offered her help or any food, just sat waiting and watching, some of the other village women circle aground the edge of the dry spit of land, hoping to throw morsel of food to her, each time, the scraps of food landed in the swamp water and were eagerly swallowed by the small animals and fort over by the insects, each time the village chief just smiled, slowly he drew another line in the mud, recording the days the old women had lasted.

Since she had returned the village area and had been banned, the usual daily life of the swamp and jungle locations had gone on, early ever day the stream of launches and boat had continued to pass the jungle villages, on both sides of the main stream of muddy water flow, as each tide forced water into the swamp areas, before ebbing out the same water flows,

With the passing of daylight to darkness she had now seen two days pass, still the village chief sat staring at the old women, she had seen the boats going to the oil platform being built only 900mtrs away. Had also seen them leaving every night before it got dark, still nothing changed, only the water at night began to feel much colder.

The small swamp creatures were now becoming bolder, scrabbling around her feet under the water, dry tears streamed down her face, her hands had also began to loose their feeling, so she tied her hand to the canoe in case she fell over. Her mind began to remember day as a little girl as she played with the other children in her home village, she felt she had been happy then, a home a family no cares or worries, until the day she had been taken, she had been only thirteen years old, remembering this time made her feel totally sad, for she now knew her time would be soon ended.

Lightness began to etch is way through the overhead canopy of the jungle trees, already warm at this early hour, again she had heard the boats coming, no longer able to stand without leaning over her canoe, she struggled to twist her head round so she could see which boat was passing, pain racked through her body, as the effort of standing in the swamp water was making her legs become weaker, her mouth started to gently foam, she called her mother, although she hardly knew who she was, to many days and years had past to remember,

She could easily feel the swamp creatures nibbling at her feet and legs, she was no longer able to making them move away, she had also seen the larger croc moving ever closer, only by moving the pole could she stop them from edging even closer, her eyes were constantly shedding tears, but none ever run down her face, the village chief remained sitting at the edge of the swamp, knowing it would not be long now before she fell off the canoe and disappear beneath the swamp water.

SAVIOUR/RESCUE

The oil companies work boat had slowed down, was edging closer to the spit of land where the kids lived, as usual it pushed nearer to the tiny spit of high ground opposite from the chiefs village, small parcels of food and sweets were thrown to the children, they scrabbled for the gifts immediately filling their mouths laughing and shouting as the boat pulled away, waving and whooping they watched as the boat moved towards the spit of high ground where the village chief sat. The local boatman shouted to the village chief, on the second call the village chief got up and walked towards the boat, a deep conversation took place, the village chief kept waving his arm back towards the old women, shaking his head each time, each time the answer was a firm shake of is head,

    The white man had listened to all of this discussion, brought up his hand and rubbed his figure and thumb together, immediately the village chief held up his hand with three fingers showing, the boatman looked at the white man, who held up one and a half fingers, tilting his head from side to side, at last the village chief smiles nodding his head, immediately the money changed hands, a short further discussion took place, one more finger was held up, his hand made a circle twice, the white man nodded, all raised their hands and clasped them together, every thing had been agreed.

    The village chief moved over to where the old women was still clinging onto the canoe, waving his arm he motioned for her to come closer, rapidly he explained to her, she could now move her canoe back to the spit of high ground, already he had called to the other village men to fetch poles and banana fronds, which they were now shaping and pushing into the semi mud surface, she still stood along side of her canoe, as though it was an item of her Independence, the small rope string still attached her to the canoe.

She had nodded off into a light sleep, when the village chief grasped her shoulder, in panic she began to struggle away from him, until he pointed to the newly build lean to shack, releasing the rope from her wrist, he led her to the building, speaking rapidly in the local dialect he explained this was now her home for as long as she lived, bewildered she stared at him, point to her chest she asked, mine, his nodding head and broad smile gave her the answer, turning he then pointed to her canoe, two village men were now pulling it away, screaming she tried to move after it, again the village chief grasped her arm, sitting her down began to explain what she had not heard, gradually her tears were replaced with a look of amazement, as he told her the white man had been extremely upset, seeing her always stood in the swamp water, so had ordered the village chief to rebuild her home and to make her a new canoe, which was now being built by the village men who fashioned canoes.

After three more days, in which the village chief now had always provided her with water and food, there was a new canoe gently floating, close to the rebuilt forest constructed home, eagerly she tried sitting in the high seat of the canoe, she noted that the canoe builders had also layered the bottom of the canoe with sweated on leaves, making the canoe even more water tight.

Her face was now always fixed with a happy broken tooth grin, never she thought had she imagined that she would be happier than when she first moved to this locations all those years ago, each morning she would wake up and would see her canoe gently bobbing in the slight movement of the jungle waters, she could now choose when to fish or maybe she would visit other swamp villages that were dotted along every creek, no more was she reliant on other villagers to be on the look out for her, in case her old canoe became flooded, never had she felt happier.

Often she would hear the boats from the oil companies passing both up and down from the platforms. She seem always to miss seeing the white mans boat go past, although she knew it had been there as the small parcel of foods was always outside of her home, no longer did the other villagers steal the food parcels, instructions had been given by the village chief, some days there were parcels, some days there were none, but always the next day there would be more parcels, now happy and more content, she often paddled her canoe down the smaller creeks to catch fish, making sure first that the crocodiles were not in sight, fishing in these small creeks was safer than the large open creeks,

Makaraba, is just nine hundred meters due east of the slightly raised land area that Sara lived on, numerous and many times she had seen and noted the boats and launches that were continually travelling up and down to Makaraba oil companies platform, some times she would shake her fist at the passing water traffic, when water from the speeding boats slopped over into her new canoe, again she would bail out the excess water before she would venture into the creeks on fishing trips, so she made a ruling that whilst they were constructing and building the Makaraba platforms she would only fish close to the swamp edges.

This would restrict what she could catch, making living life even more restrictive, throughout and often during these fishing trips, she would glimpse movement of boats, usually with many workers on board, though they never appeared to see her, as she always now kept close to the banks of the swamp, clearly she could often see these foreigners, always she felt lonely, none of these people would wave or acknowledge her, even when they sometimes passed close to where she was fishing, always they would chase and scatter any fish away.

MAKARABA FATALITY

Slowly throughout the day local gossip stories began to filter out and spread, all of the activity early that day had been due to one of the construction team from the Makaraba platform had fallen into the swamp waters, being totally drunk he had been unable to clamber back onto the rigging around the platform,

Later it was rumored that because the main oil company had completed their on shore connections for the platform hook up, had been completed successfully, the companies employees had celebrated with a full blown party, which had lasted over seven hours, the engineer who had fallen off the platform, had lived in another section of the accommodation, which was over a small high bridge walkway, that coupled the two platform sections together, scuff marks of this bridging section indicated that he had fallen cutting his self as he fell, before landing in the swamp waters.

He had, as now had been established, left the celebration party, drunkenly staggering across the main platform decking, until he reached the cross over bridge, being unable to see clearly, he had tried to grasp the flimsy hand rail on the cross over bridge, missing it, had fallen striking his head knocking his self out, blood (which was later found) had spilt down dripping into the water, recovering slightly, he had pulled his self up onto his knees.

Due to his extreme lack of control for body movement, he never shouted or made any noises that would have alerted his co-workers, scrabbling around whilst kicking out his feet, managed at last to attain a standing position, but his drunken state had kept him unbalanced, as he over balanced again, he grabbed the bridge rail chain, before tumbling down into the murky swamp waters, flesh from his hand, would be found days later, the blood dripping from his previous injuries, that had dropped into the swamp waters, had already alerted the waiting colonies of crocodiles.

After an investigation that lasted two days, it was confirmed that this engineer had been taken by the crocodiles, that always swam close to the platform during hours of darkness, the management of the contracting oil company, then authorized the companies employee's loss of life compensation scheme, compensating his wife with the compensation insurance that was provided, through his employment as a contracting worker, a week after he went missing some of his clothing was found floating in the swamp waters.

CANOEING HAPPYNESS

None of this obviously registered or affected Sara, as she continued her own daily struggle for life as only she knew it, through his illness the man she lived with had progressively become weaker, being unable to take the canoe out on fishing trips, leaving every thing for her to do, with his health being more pronounced she had also to tend and feed him, some times washing him, when he could not move.

But nothing on the companies platform activities effected her and her living with resourcing things and food that only her and her man relied on, the tragic loss of the life of the engineer did affected her, because she knew that these creatures were always within the surrounding waters of the swamps, therefore and unfortunately, even after the loss of the platform engineer, the company or local communities, did not post any warnings or suggested to all personnel that they employed with regards to these hazardous happenings, thereby each and any day or when Sara was in need of food supplies, she would set off paddling down through the creeks, into the main water ways, around Jones Creek.

TROPICAL STORM FISHING

The main water expanse of Jones Creek was not to the liking of the jungle dwelling local villagers, who only existed around the edges of these vast expanses of open tidal river swamp waters. Now because the late afternoon and evening breezes had got up, rippling the surface with small breaking waves, making it difficult to paddle across the cross breeze expanses of the open waters, knowing they could risk the canoes filling with spray from the wavelets of water.

Sara would often creep along the sides of the stretches of open water as she navigated throughout the water creek systems, in fear of water entering her canoe, mostly though she would think about the bigger and larger crocodiles that were always present in the denser and habitable area's of the swamp masses of mangrove tree routes, these usually were the area's where these reptiles laid their eggs and after hatching would give good care to their young.

She had often seen the white mans boat cruising around the open stretches of water, mostly to far away to be able to see her against the back drop of the tangled masses of mangrove roots, she had always raised her paddle, maybe he would see it, but always he would disappear racing either up towards Makaraba or in the other direction towards Upamami, quickly his launch would disappear in a cloud of spray.

Every day in her travels through the creeks and swamp streams, she would often call at small enclaves of civilization that bordered the swamps, some times gleaming nuggets of information from these creek side villages, often just daily chit-chat, so it was a major talking point when the village chiefs suddenly held a meeting, calling in other creek side village chiefs, to discuss the latest whispers from the swamp villages, which brought back the horror of the Makaraba engineer being taken by the crocodile.

RAPE

On that particular same day, one of the young women girls at the Makaraba location had been taken, by a local national worker, hired by the oil company, into the area's near swamp, and savagely raped this young girl. Whilst the uproar over the missing companies platform engineer was still in the throws of ongoing, by all other employees and employers, who had been searching the length and breath of the surrounding swamp area's.

The local Nigerian employee had noticed a young village girl, roaming around the edges of the dry spit of land, it appeared she was out collecting sticks and small branches for firewood, as he was watching her wander around, not knowing she was being watched by anyone, she had bent down to pick up some small sticks.

It was then that the local employee had noticed she wore no underwear, as she came closer, she again bent over collecting more sticks, the local Nigerian employee became intensely inflamed with instant desire, quickly slipping off of the oil platform, he began to slowly follow the young girl, each time she stopped to pick up small sticks, his inflamed urges pushed him closer to the young girl, finally as she entered the bush trees that surrounds the swamp edges, he grabbed the young girl quickly, over powering her, before spreading her legs open and raping her, she had as she was grabbed, managed to let out a piercing scream, his rape actions did not last very long, so after clambering up off the swamp floor, he aim a kick at the young girl, the young girl avoided the flying boot, before she grabbed his leg and sunk her teeth into the fleshy part of his leg, this inflamed him again, so pulling the young girl back towards him, he turned her over and again savagely raped her from the rear, she was crying and sobbing as he again discarded her into the swamp bush's, before rushing deeper into the swamp bush roots.

The Nigerian Naval guards who afforded the security to the oil companies platforms had heard the first piercing scream, taking note of where it had come from, seeing nothing moving, they lost interest, as they again turned their attention to the ongoing search for the missing companies platform engineer, until again they heard shouting and screaming at the jungle swamp edge, moving quickly towards the noise and movement, and the now clear sobbing sounds, they found the young girl laying on the swamp ground, quickly she told the naval guards what had happened, as she scrambled to her feet, suddenly there was thrashing and shouting in the swamp bush's, as three local villagers dragged out the local village companies employee, who still had his private parts huge out, already they had placed a rope around his neck, pulling and pushing him along the faint path towards the local village, they too had heard the screams and noises, so had followed the sounds, finally come upon the local Nigerian employee discarding the young girl as he finished with her.

Arriving at the swamp village main area, the villagers had placed a thick plank of wood, over two tree trunks, laying the local Nigerian company employee along the board, they had placed a smaller thin log across his elbow joints under the plank, then tied his hand above him waist, so he was totally beyond movement, they had also taken his penis and testicles, strapping them onto the board he was laid on, with another rope around his neck, stretching him along the board, restricting him from any movement what so ever, the village chief and the local villagers, who had captured him were now arguing, as to whether to castrate him first or behead him, then castrate him, pointing the long bladed hacking knives, at these specific area's as they argued.

The first of the naval guards to arrive, fired his rifle into the air, it was his only bullet, as the naval guards had to pay for their bullets, the village chief and the villagers stopped all movement, as the second guard arrived pointing his rifle at the villagers group, having heard the shouting and the noise of the capture, the commander of the naval guards had also followed.

RAPIST ARRESTED

The commander of the naval guards moved quickly towards the tied down Nigerian company employee, standing over him he began to release the restricted prisoner, this caused the village chief to raise his hacking blade, pointing it towards the naval commander, the second naval guard aimed his rifle at the village chief, only he knew that he could not fire his rifle, for he had no bullet in the rifle, seeing this, the village chief immediately backed off, allowing the naval commander to free the tied up prisoner, handing over a note that the naval commander had written, all the naval personnel began to move towards their boat,

SARA'S FEARS

Sara had since the white man became involved, often roamed around the masses of creeks and minor tributaries throughout the local area's of the swamp's, never had she considered going further than the creeks and lakes she knew, always fearful of the stories and the many mentions of the length and size of the monster crocodile, that swam through the higher reaches of the densest sections of the wildest swamps, even thinking of these area's made her shudder with outright fear. In her mind she thought about the companies platform engineer, feeling very sad that whilst enjoying his self, he had tragically lost his life, shuddering even more she tried to concentrate on what she was doing, knowing she could not do any thing about it did not remove it from her mind, gently paddling down the Makaraba creek, the naval guards launch sped past her, heading down the creek towards Warri, although she had only recently heard about the rape of the young girl at Makaraba, she wished it had been the Nigerian platform worker, who had been fallen foul to the crocodile, under her breath she cursed him, wishing him evil.

GATHERING STORM CLOUDS

Sara must have fallen asleep, for when she opened her eyes the Jones Creek lake waters were flat calm, not a ripple showed on the surface, turning her head thought she noted large black clouds gathering over the distant jungle trees, suddenly she heard distant thunder, which rolled around the jungle mangrove swamp, sounding far away as yet, she made haste to untie her canoe, wanting to be on her way should the presenting storm come nearer, she had noted that she had tied up four miles short of the Makaraba out flow channel, so this left her with a at least two hours of paddling before she could enter into the Makaraba creek, back to where she had lived all her life, pulling a bit harder on her paddle she tried op speed up this time.

ARREST MOVEMENT

The navy guards managed to haul their prisoner into their transfer launch, setting off down the Makaraba creek, the village boss man waved the piece of paper the guards had given him, moving down the banks at the side of the creek, stopping the launch the navy guards, edged into the banking, shouting to the village chief, holding up two fingers, indicating they would be back in two days time, mollified the village boss turn away.

SARA'S FATALITY

She felt it rather than saw it, the tropical storm suddenly had filled the complete sky, black dark dense cloud base was registering only just above the water level, rolling thunder boomed throughout the length and breath of the oncoming storm, lighting strikes fizzled from the storm clouds, striking with load explosions into the water near to where she was, driving her off of her preset route, never had she seen a storm like this, she dare not try to stand up as her head would have been inside of the thundering cloud. Pulling hard on her paddle was all she could do, even though she did not appear to move, but little by little her canoe crept slowly forward, mangrove swamp trees edged past, no long could she see where she was going, suddenly the mangrove trees were gone, smaller fern fan leaved trees took their place, the surface of the swamp water became slightly flatter, then she realized she had wandered into a small creek off of the main swamp creeks.

Visibly shaken Sara began to back paddle her canoe, struggling to move its length around in her efforts to exit the small creek. Although paddling with much effort, she could not make the canoe turn or back up, then she saw a huge fish flash over the waters surface, joyously her mood changed, with a fish that size it would last her weeks. She began to pull the netting and fishing line moving the recovered netting and line into the canoes bottom, bracing her feet against the canoe side, she gradually began to haul the fish towards the canoe side, struggling against the weight of the fish, she managed one huge effort, that brought the fish half in and half out of the canoe, bending over she grabbed the fishes tail, which began to roll the fish into her canoe, with her effort and her mind on retrieving this fish, she had failed to notice the small V shape cruising towards her canoe, with a sudden flash of its head and half of its body, the huge crocodile snapped its jaws over both the half in, half out fish, along with a large section of her canoe, twisting as its jaws closed, breaking off a long section of her canoe, with half of the fish which still hung from its shut jaw, Sara had been flipped out of the canoe through the efforts of the crocodile, she had landed over ten feet from the now half flooded canoe, scrabbling across the water surface she managed to reach the half flooded canoe, through shear effort she began to haul herself back into the canoe, now lying half in half out of the canoe, the crocodile returned, speeding towards the canoe, clamping its jaws over her still hung out legs, whilst twisting several times, screaming Sara clung desperately onto the other side of the canoe, through shear effort she hung on until the final twist of the crocodile tore the skin and flesh from her body, gulping the severed leg into its blood dripping jaw, before flipping the severed leg into its jaw and throat.

AS SARA STRUGGLED AGAINST THE CROCODILE, ONLY FIVE MILES DISTANCE AWAY AT THE RIVER SIDE OF THE SWAMP.

RIVER SWAMP RESCUE

The launch carrying the white man, along with the daily change over crews, were having extreme difficulties, in finding or locating the entrance to the jungle creeks, as the tropical storm cloud base was very low, just standing up, put the crews heads into the cloud base, consequently every one had to crouch over, in order to see where they were going, torrential rain squalls lashed rain in blinding sheets, blotting out normal vision, fierce thunder blasts and lightening flashes also did not help. But now inside of the swamp creek system, they made their way towards the next marked entrance, between the slightly visible reed beds.

Faintly between the crashes of thunder and the brilliant lightening flashes which decrease visibility drastically a piecing scream caused the crew to look around, against the backdrop of the reed screen two local canoes were silhouetted in the flashing lightening, could be made out, two local tribes women were splashing water out of the canoes which were already heavily laden with wooden logs, trying to keep them afloat, but rapidly were loosing the battle, the white man pointed to the canoes, the Nigerian boatman eased the launch slowly towards the two canoes, the canoe piled high with logs of timbers collected by the women.

Each had a child sat on top of the wood, as the launch neared the first canoe, the screaming woman pick up the child, her efforts rocked the canoe, which immediately turned over, dumping all of the wood into the swamp, with both the child and the woman both disappeared under the water.

SARA'S LONELY BATTLE

Sara had finally fell into the half flooded canoe, dragging herself into the flooded water, began to bail out the canoe, she searched around trying to find where the crocodile was, not seeing it, she continue bailing out the excess water, before attempting to try to paddle the canoe into the Makaraba creek waterway, agonizingly slowly whilst sobbing huge running tears, she began to head towards the spit of land she called home.

SWAMP WATER REED BED RESCUES

Observing what was happening, the white man immediately dived over the launches side, pushing aside the half sunken wood logs, he made out the small arm of the young child, grabbing the child arm, he pushed back to the surface, hoisting the child over the side of the launch, dip diving again towards the reed bed edge, he made out the struggling form of the local woman, grasping her arm he pulled her to the surface, the launch was now twenty five meters away, but was coming towards him, placing his arm on the edge of the launch he heaved her aboard. The Nigerian boatman was pointing away from him, so holding onto the launches edge, the launch dragged him towards the other heavily loaded second local canoe, shouting at the local woman to throw all the wood out of the canoe. The launch began to close towards the canoe, again the, woman tried to throw the child onto the launch, the launch which was still moving, pushed the child away from the edge of the launch, this was seen by the white man, who plucked the child out of the swamp water and threw him over arm into the boat, as the other canoe began to sink the woman pushed away from the sinking canoe, now naked to the waist through her efforts of off loading the wooden sticks, she thrashed towards the white man, who grasped her wrist as she came nearer, dragging her towards the launch which had been edging closer, grasping the launch edge with one hand he hoisted her into the launch, where she flopped onto the the launches deck.

RESCUED DELIVERANCE

Through his efforts and having retrieved the local women from the swamp, as he had pushed her into the launch, he noted and had seen a small rope around her wrist, pulling this from her arm, he began to pull the rope, the local women canoe boobed to the surface empty of the wooden logs, passing the rope up to the Nigerian launches driver he was pulled aboard, making sure the rope and canoe were tied tight, the launch made its way back to the villagers home, deeper into the swamp, on the only dry spit of land around.

The arrival of the launch at the villagers camp caused a considerable uproar, as the rescued villagers ran into the tribal section of their village, excitedly describing their rescue experience to the other villagers, many voices could be heard shouting followed by cheering, whole sections of the village people began to rush towards the launch, bringing with them much food and large jugs of drink.

The white man ordered the launch to back off, as soon as the villagers were safely on the dry spit of land, so as they rushed back to the launch, it was more than 40 meres away, the crew and workers all waved as the launch began to turn and speed away, the lamenting shout of the villagers grew loader as the complete village population stood begging the launch to return. Signaling to the boatman the white man ordered the launch to continue towards Odidi, the first platform manned by the operators in the launch, as the launch disappeared through the reed curtain, the shouting of the villagers still followed the launch.

SARA'S AGONISING JOURNEY HOME

After two hours she still had more than another mile to go, the effort of moving the canoe with the large paddle was taking its toll, slower and slower she began to move it into the creek edges, forcing her to use up more of her depleting strength, throughout all of this time the faint vie shape had been behind her, stopping only when she stopped paddling, until finally she reach the land space of her home, pushing again on the heavy paddle she aimed for her home area making the last desperate effort she could, of finally bringing her now broken canoe, to the spit of land she called home.

SARA'S FAIRWELL

The village chief had since she finally came into sight, been watching the events as they happened, he had seen the narrow movement behind the damaged canoe, quickly gathering the other villagers around him, began to throw small branches over Sara head, in an effort of distracting the now appearing crocodile, twisting her head Sara could see what the village chief was throwing the small branches at, Sara screamed a long piercing scream, which some how hung in the the heat laden air, lunging the crocodile shot forward again snapping its jaws onto the rear of the canoe, flipping Sara high over its body length into the swamp water behind where she had come from, before sinking beneath the muddied swamp waters.

The village chief and villagers stood watching, the swirling swamp waters had flattened out, as one the villagers started to turn away, the waters erupted around the surfacing crocodile, Sara was half in the jaws of the crocodile and half out, as they all watched, a second eruption of swamp water showed another crocodile lunging towards the first crocodile, clamping its jaws across Sara dangling body, both crocodiles then rolled away from each other, stretching her frail body between then, with a terrifying crack her body at last parted, each crocodile falling back under the swamp water, small wavelets cascaded onto the shore, before rippling back into the swamp waters, suddenly as the watching crowd had thought the tragic scene over, the crocodile rolled again, as it did so, Sara's arm and hand broke the surface, stunned they all watched as the hand and arm ached in beckoning wave, before slowly slipping into the swamp waters, horrified the village chief and the villagers shrank back away from the carnage they had just witnessed, Sara canoe now spun away from the spit of land, badly damaged it began to fill with water, gradually sinking as it joined the main stream swamp water flows.

RAPIST DELIVERED

The naval guards small launch had arrived with the local Nigerian prisoner, still handcuffed, at the main naval headquarters in Warri, immediately as the crime story was being related, policemen and bystanders would attack the cuffed prisoner, so by the time he was officially handed into the care of the police station, he was covered in blood from many cuts and bruises, the headquarter inspector refused to place him in front of the local Nigerian magistrate for fear that in his beat up state, they would release him, due to his injuries, thereafter due to another frenzied attack, he was kept in the cell block under guard.

HONOURING SARA'S LIFE

The village people along with the village chief had stood throughout the disappearing spectacle unable to move, frozen at the horrifying heart stopping scenes they had just witnessed, they were all transfixed unable to look away from the spot where Sara had finally disappeared, shoulder shaking whilst tears streamed down over their checks, until the village chief let out a terrifying scream, falling to his knees, beating the heated baked mud with his fists, again and again, making a low moaning sound, finally he raised his self up, ordering two of the village women to destroy Sara's home, instructing them to remove every thing, moving it across the patch of muddy jungle space that was the home to them all, where the fire still burned, discarding every thing into the flames, not speaking until these tasks were complete, then instructing the two women to place his chief's chair, next to Sara's previous home space before seating down, he knew the white man would be back again, but when, so he would await his arrival.

RUNNING UNDER THE TROPICAL STORM

Although at this time, after the savage spectacle of the final throws of Sara's life, because and due only to distance, the white man had returned back his rig platform, after his terrifying rescue efforts on the other side of the swamp area, the tropical storm had raged most of the day, closing down any day light, that had struggled to appear, he had then decided to return all other workers back to Warri, as the torrential rain still was pouring down, one of the launches made its way to Makaraba, the white man set off down Jones Creek, towards the secondary section of the Warri river, the storm clouds were so low, they were only literally feet above the river water, both the bosun and the white man, peering under the cloud base to see where they were going, suddenly the bosun slowed the launch down, stating to the white man, "boss, we have left the creek", the white man, just pointed and indicated, straight on, huge rumbling cracks of thunder rumbled around, lightening flashes, erupted all around the small craft, distantly, but could not be seen, lightening bolts were striking the water, whilst still trying to peer through a wall of water, the bosun and the white man were totally drenched to the skin.

Raising his head slightly the white man pointed ahead, both could just make out the dark edge of the far shore line, indicating with his left arm the white man brought the launch to turn away from the now visible shore line, a huge bolt of lightening flashed into the water, three feet behind the now speeding launch, rolls of thunder still rattled the launch and the water around the launch, glancing back to where the bolt of lightening had landed, the white man look up before saying "that was close, but you missed". His bosun was a very religious believer, begged the white man, "please boss do not upset, him, he may do it again, we has motor spirit in those cans at the back of the boat", as the bosun finished speaking another huge bolt of lightening, hit the river water inches away from the launch, casually the white man looked around, then turning his head towards the cloud base, he said "O.K you have made your point, I apologize, unreservedly.

Suddenly the sky cleared, all the clouds were gone, the sky was brilliantly blue, and there was no wind, the river waters were total flat and calm, the white man looked at the bosun who was still praying, touching his arm, the bosun still with his hand held in the praying position, raised his head before saying, thank you God. Indicating the spectacular view now before them, they carried on the Warri sailing through the brilliant sun shine.

Glancing back to where they had come from, the terrifying black storm cloud could still be seen, diminishing into the distance.

PRISONER MOVEMENT

Each new relay of naval guards were restricted from the cell block, the inspector and the duty desk officer took to leaving the cell block entrance door open, in fear of further prisoner beatings against this particular prisoner, finally he had been before the magistrate, who sent him to be tried at the law courts in Lagos, transporting him in a cramped police van, his treatment during this journey was to be laid on the floor, whilst the accompanying police officers kept him under foot, he received further beatings as he was booked in when the charges were read out, hand cuffed, then thrown into a cell, meal times they would chain him to the wall, by one hand, only allowing him to access his food with the other.

DISTRUPTION OF WORKERS

With the days work coming to its end, the naval commanders launch arrived at the yet to be completed platform, they shouted for the white man to come back to the base camp, requesting to know why, they just indicated that the naval commander had requested the white man to come.

On arrival at the base camp jetties, every one of the 450 local and expat employees were milling around, shouting and screaming at each other, with the naval commanders aid, they separated the groups of employees, the white man then requested each group leader what their problem was, as each gave their answers, the white man sent each group back to their rooms, leaving only their leaders, reducing the crowd from 450, down to twelve people, further questioning revealed the main problem, two of the live in Nigerian girls had created an argument, between them, which had got out of hand.

Having the two girls brought onto the jetty head, the white man instructed the rest of the contractors to return to their rooms, but the two girls would remain on the jetty head, until the white man returned. On his return the white man questioned the two girls, finally getting to the truth, he allowed the innocent girl to return to her sleeping room, but ordered the naval guards to move the other girl to their barracks room, all naval guards were now broadly smiling, as under their Nigerian punishment rules, they would thrash the naked bodies of people who had committed any crime, with their thick webbing buckled belts, following the girl and the guards into the barrack room, the guards were already stripping belts ready for use.

The white man stopped them, deflated they asked why, smiling to his self, the white man said, "tell her and inform this girl, if she does not agreed and accept what I am going to state, she will be taken immediately to "Berritt Island". On hearing this the naval guards exploded into rocking laughter jigging around their barrack room, informing the girl of these rules, the girl collapsed onto the floor, begging the white man not to send her to the Island, he simple stated, "should you again cause any disruption any more, you will go".

The white man then instructed the naval guards to return the girl back to her room, ordering them to return with the other girl, both guards were still grinning, with the other girl now before him the white had the naval guards tell the girl in their local language (Ibo) what would happen to either or both girls, should they wish continue their personal dispute with each other. The naval guards could not contain their selves, telling every one what would happen should "any" girl caused problems.

BERRITT ISLAND

By the next morning word of what had happened, was all over the swamp "bush telegraph", Walter the total project engineer, from Warri contacted the white man, simply saying "problem", the answer from the white was one worded, "no", came the reply, "will leave it with you then" stated Walter. All the other platform managers, made contact with the white man, requiring to know about Berritt Island, deflecting each enquiry, the white man stated a time within the next two weeks, where they would all meet up, he would then explain, what and where Berritt Island was, also adding, they really should not go there, better they dropped the subject.

    Two weeks later, the five other platform managers turned up at Jones Creek platform, they wished and requested the white man to escort them to Berritt Island, after explaining to the other managers, what Berritt Island was used for and where it was, made them all more determined to go, therefore the six launch's set out for the Island. Arriving at the Berritt Island location, each launch dropped its cargo of a manager, onto the flimsy jetty, as they all made their way along the precarious flimsy jetty, the other managers expressed their concern, "where is the Island", the white man now laughing, spread his arms out, whilst saying "this is it, there is no Island, just this wooden flimsy wooden structure", indicating it was above the water, so it was an Island, also explaining to the others,"that is sinking sands, covered with sea snakes and sea water crocodiles, any one coming here is kept here until their time has been served", "unless they have boats or launch's, consequently, "its an Island". Later on the white man would get the Island manager to describe the incident of the previous years, to the other managers, maybe then they would fully understand. By now the residence girls had seen the launch's arrive and were now making their way along the jetties flimsy foot path, the white man had sent his launch driver into Warri, to collect the white mans, Mr Fix it, five of the girls had hooked their arms through the other managers arms, another two girls were each trying to join up with each man, the white man carried on walking towards the Island keeper of Berritt Island, none of the girls tried to hook up with him.

Greeting the Island keeper, the white man circled his hand, every one received a bottle of beer, the girls all roared with laughter, during a lull of the laughter, the white man requested the Island manager, to relate his story of the two girls, who had wished to leave, glancing around the other managers, he began his story, two girls who had been on the Island for nearly three months, had arrange between their selves, to get off the Island. They fashioned two feet long boards, made holes through which they lace pieces of rope, when all of the girls had began to fall asleep, they clambered down onto the sand wearing their flat wooden laced boards, whist they continued to slowly move one foot in front of the other, their progress, was maintained, from his look out point on the Island, he could see they had made their way half way to the shore line, they had not looked back, just continued to slide one foot before the other, but suddenly one of the girls had seen the sea snakes, screaming at the other girl, she had stopped, as did the girl with her, because now they had stopped, the walking boards began to sink, sand spilled over the top of the boards, although both girls were still screaming, they tried to lift their feet, with the boards fully covered with sand they both fell over, as he watched, the Island manager saw the the two girls, sink under the sand, spreading his hands, he asked "what could I do", a small tear fell from his eye, "so I tell all girls, just do your time, and be safe". The sombre looks that had been on the girls faces, as he relayed his story, were now gone, as they again targeted, each of the platform managers, who had three girls each trying to grab and hold their body parts, as fast as one was pushed aside, the other two succeeded in grasping sections the first had not got too, the white man glanced over at this never ending loss of dignity, raising an eyebrow, casually asking "enough", all managers agreed, the white man glanced at the Island keeper, slightly shook his head, immediately all the girls stopped, standing back, as though they were not interested.

"Did you just do that", one of the managers said, glancing at the speaker, the white man smiled, "you cannot control these people" said the one who had asked, the white man again glancing at the Island manager, all the girls began to molest the others, "bloody hell" said the speaker, "it was you", looking up at his Mr Fix it, the white man moved his head towards the speaker, immediately one of the girls stepped up, taking the mans hand, lead him away, all activity from the girls also had stopped, circling his hand again, other bottles of beer was past round to every one, twenty minutes later the first critical speaker returned with the girl, only this time, there was a slight smile on his face, leaning close to the white man, he whispered "you b**tard", smiling the white man shrugged his shoulders, to which the other manager said "but it was nice, no penetration", every one cracked out laughing. The white man looked at his Mr Fix it, who rubbed his fingers together, 255 Nira, "all" stated the white man, a head nod agreed, indicating they were now leaving, the white again made a circular movement, increasing the money required, them placed another 100 Nira onto the offered bill, suddenly all the girls whooped with laughter as they realized he had bought them another beer each. As the launches sailed away, all the girls shouted and screamed after them, until the launches could not be seen.

CONFORMATION AND AGREEMENT

Since Sara's demise had taken place, the village chief still waited, sat on his seat, alongside Sara's old living site, they fed him they gave him drinks, but stoically he remained seated staring into the swamp waters, each day the boats and launches swept passed, but the white man's launch never appeared, the village chief would at times slump forward, as tiredness became to much for him, sagging forward in his seat, sometimes falling out of the seat, before staggering back up to re-seat his self. On the forth day of this procedure the white mans launch appeared, immediately on seeing that Sara home was not there, cruised up to the raised spit of jungle muddy land, on demand from the white man, the village chief explained in his local dialect to the launch coxswain, what had happened to Sara, as he finished tears were streaming down his face, from his sash around his waist he extracted the money notes, the white man had given him for Sara, waving this offer away the white man, asked the launch coxswain to request the village chief for a further request, in his local dialect, the Nigerian coxswain described the final farewell, the white man had requested for Sara, the white man wanted the village chief to carry out for the white man, when it was explained to the village chief, his face had a look of amazement, readily he agreed, only stating the white man brought the items that had been requested, four hours later these items were delivered.

FATALITY COMPENSATION

When the naval guards had delivered their prisoner to the lock up in Warri, their commander had informed the oil companies on site bosses, this created a international problem, as the home office management in Germany were less than happy, instructions were given to negotiate with the Makaraba village chief, on compensation of the young girls family, under the companies policy of recompense for physical contact frustration to the local community. Thereafter the village chief was transported to the Warri head office, discussions then took place to decide the amount to be paid for the young girls trauma, finally a figure was agreed, the company would compensate the local family by paying 177,000 Nira. In his calculations the village chief had used this figure, indicating to the oil company officers, that he would only take 10% of this total, as his payment for the negotiations on behalf of the family, insisting that the hand over of the money sum's would take place on the Makaraba platform, monitored by the oil companies on site field engineer, the village chief receiving his take, whilst the family would receive the balance.

With this sum of money being handed over to the local village chief, the company decided it must being handled through the correct procedures, therefore they nominated their civil swamp food and water supplying engineering manager, Paul Stricker, as their official representative who would conduct the companies acknowledgement, of their Nigerian workers wrong doing, for his critical crime against the child from their village, for which he was now being punished through the courts, thereafter handing over the money paid out by the oil company, directly to the villagers, on board the Makaraba gas production platform, these agreed instructions were relaid to the village chief along with a printed copy, which would be handed to the village chief on completion of the ceremony, when the money was to be given to the young girls family.

SARA'S LIFE LEGACY

Sara had throughout her life, during all the years she had spent living and surviving every thing the area, location and swamp had caused her difficulties and hardship over these eons of years, never had she been accorded any recompense or compensation for all the times the companies launches and work boasts, had swamped the living spit of land, that the villagers lived on, although the village chief constantly took trips to remonstrate with the oil companies platform manager, who would issue instructions to the work boat drivers to slow down as they passed these habitat area's, never did they keep up this request, some times when the speeding launches and boats would wash their wakes up onto the spit of land, making it very difficult to relaunch them back into the water, always she would have to seek help from the other village dwellers, cutting her time she could fish or find food for them both when her man had been alive, always she would shake her fist at these speeding boats, but it never stopped them, later or the next day they would again race past.

PRISONER ESCAPE

In the criminal court Lagos, the trial day had arrived, still only dressed in the cloths he had been caught in, they stank, having only been allowed to wash twice, he was lead into the central court, handcuffed to the rail of the chair, before the judge made his entrance, the court councillor read out the charges, rape of a village minor, rape of female girl of younger tender age, molesting of a women under age of a minor, then repeating the same offence against the same young girl. The judge peered out over the court, any one standing for the defence, he asked casually, a young man stood up, he was dressed in a black suite, suitable for a young lawyer, looking up at the at the judge, I am your honour.

With the stare of the judge still registering in his the mind, the young lawyer, began to answer the charges as previously read out by the courts usher, guilty on all charges your honour, guilty as charged, sitting back the judge intoned, this then shorten all procedures for this trial, with no case or charges to answer, it only remains for me to sentence the accused, at a later day. Thank you your honour, stated the young lawyer sitting back down, have the prisoner stand urged the judge, you will be kept locked up, until the courts have set a final judgement on you, stated the judge, take him away.

Before leading the prisoner away, the court's policemen had to unlock the handcuffs from the chair arm rail, at the sound of snick as the release mechanism open, the prisoner charged forward, catching both guards unaware, knocking them both to the floor, already leaping over the guards who were struggling in a heap on the floor, he bound down the steps, to the cell block which was completely unguarded, the outside door appeared open, glancing around this door, no one was there, so walking out, he joined the thronged crowd of ever day pedestrians, who where roaming the streets outside, suddenly he was lost in the crowd, casually glancing back he could see the prison offices scanning the crowds for him, holding his nerve, desperately stopping his self from running, moved slowly further and further away, no one shouted, no one was running towards him, they were in fact starting to look the other way.

AS TIME MOVES ON

The white man had since Sara's unfortunate tragic end, continued to travel widely throughout the swamp area's, always reminding each days change over crews to drop off at the swamp side villages, little parcels of foods and sweets, the village children would leap and shout as the companies launches and boats moved up and down the swamp creeks, stationed now more often at Jones Creek, most rig work traffic moving throughout the swamps, would usually anchor up at Jones Creek, consequently this area became a hub for outlying visitors and the local nearby villages, its preference became even greater as the white man introduced ice cold beer at the mid day break time, enlisting the other oil companies to supply the local bush bars with dustbins full of ice blocks every day.

Whilst the work over rig boats were anchored at Jones Creek, the white man had then install a power cable system, rigging out each jungle residence with cable power lines giving electric light for the first time ever to these isolated villagers, also with the adjacent gas platform only being 105 meters away he also had a cable laid from the rig platform, under the swamp water, to the distribution point at the Jones Creek village, recently installed powering source. Enterprising bush bar owners then bought electrical fridges, and some even bought freezers, due to the constant uninterrupted power supply, obviously drawing more peoples to the area, this measure also expanded Jones Creek as a vital village.

With his reputation becoming the talking point of the area's population, the white man had continued with his normal duties, which took his to all locations throughout the swamp land area's, returning every evening to the Jones Creek area, a visit from the local community caused him to contact the companies head office in Warri, the community had requested the company to allow the white man to become and be the local area communities area "mayor" and become the villages local magistrate, whilst he was was within these area's, it was agreed by the companies management, with the ruling it did not infringe on his companies work load and ethics, these terms and conditions were carried out, throughout his stay at Jones Creek.

RIVER RESCUE

Because of the companies progression ownership changes, having now placed the completed platforms into the hands of the clients, (Nigerian Petroleum Company), the construction company had shut down all of their jungle swamp base camps, which resulted in every day the change over crews would have to daily travel from Warri every morning, whilst having to complete the return journey back every evening.

Reaching the tributary tie in connection to the main river waterways, the whites launch was met with an unusual sight, a very large drilling rig platform was passing the entry point, this platform rig was 200mtrs long, 20mtrs high and 15mtrs wide, slowing down so as not to enter the disturbed wash water, which was leaving a four to six foot wash, it was suddenly noted that there was a very small speed boat/launch being tossed around in this disturbed water wash wake area, indicating to the coxswain, the white man had him plunge into this turbulent white water, bringing his launch up along side of this craft, the four occupants were sat cowed at the rear of the cockpit, whilst the flimsy light speed craft, bounced around in the work over rigs turbulent wake, with no one trying to control it. Standing on the edge of his launch, the white stepped across and into the cockpit of the wildly bouncing speed boat, dropping down behind the crafts wheel and levers, glancing up he could see the captain of the rig craft standing watching his every movement, he immediately flicked the steering wheel to the left, also increasing the crafts speed, as he broke away from the turbulent water edging towards the next breaking water wash, the white man held his hand up moving it forward, a toot on the rigs wheel house siren told him that the rig skipper had seen this move, as the surge on the wake grew, the white man swiftly turned right, bringing the small craft closer to the platform rigs side, before again flicking the wheel hard to the left, raising his hand again, he closed his fish, before pulling his arm back, the rigs siren again tooted, cresting the outer edges of the wash wake, he swiftly turned the wheel right, whilst gunning the engines to the maximum, surging back across the top of the wake, before plunging down into the well of the water trough wake, the white man now stood up, quickly glancing along the length of the rigs side, he again raised his arm leaving his hand open, but moving it forward, the toot of the siren showed the skipper had acknowledged this move, racing to the left as the wash wake increased, with the small craft at nearly 35% angle, the four other occupants screamed loudly, at the bottom of the trough, which was now the largest trough, he again flicked the steering wheel fully to the right, cresting the large trough, bringing the craft immediately to within three quarters of the overall length of the rig, glancing up to the bridge house, he made a circle motion to the skipper, the siren again tooted, the white man hesitated as he watched the rigs breaking wash, before dropping the small craft immediately in front of the massive rig bows, pushing the speed levers to the limits, there was total panic from the other occupants, as the rig reared up behind them, the white man did not even glance back, but began to edge the small speed craft slowly to the left, now in undisturbed clear water, the crafts propellers pushed the craft forward increasing its speed, the American skipped began tooting the siren as he saw the small craft appear from under the front of the rigs bows, speeding away, taking a huge sweep away from the platform rig, the small craft began to follow the platform rig, by a distance, still tooting the American skipper raised his hand waving to the white man, indicating by using hand signal semaphore language, the white man spelt out "thanks", the American skipper, tooted by siren three short blasts, followed by three long blasts, then again three short blasts, which spelt out, S.O.S.

The white mans own launch now closed up to the oddly shape small craft, as it came along side, the white man stepped off, into his launch, before turning to the occupants of the craft, requesting to know who they were and what company they worked for, all of the occupants, tried to talk at the same time, pointing to one, he informed the white man, they were from Shell Petroleum Company, they had wanted to cruise around the river, and yes, none of them had any experience of boats or craft, the white man, stated to them, "if you again want to cruise around, do not cross shipping traffic lanes, next time you may not be so lucky", they all expressed their gratitude, thanking the white for his help, his final words to them was, "stay on your side of the river, or if your are not competent don't do it". Making sure there were not other craft going up or down the river, the small craft made its way back across the river, but at a lot lower speed.

Two days later, Walter, the project director arrived at Jones Creek, locating the white man, he asked him what had taken place on the river near to Warri, smiling the white man stated "idiots speeding around in minute small launch" also "not understanding any river traffic knowledge", "but trying to out race one of those drilling rigs, by cutting in to close, to the water wash flows". "Good job you turned up then", Walter said whilst laughing, "how did you acquire that sort of knowledge", asked Walter, "military, three years air sea rescue, in the north sea", stated the white man, shaking his hand Walter informed the white man, congratulations from the company, for rescuing those people, a mere gentle nod of his head, was the white mans acknowledgement.

A further week later, whilst the white man and the construction team was on lunch break at the local bush bar, opposite the platform, a helicopter landed at the Shell site helipad, soon afterwards, a Shell launch arrived at the bush bar, the white mans Mr Fix it stood up in front of the white man, the new arrival asked "where is the white man", moving his Mr Fix it man aside, the white man stood up, grasping the extended hand, saying "that will be me then", indicating towards the Shell area, the man stated, "I am from the Shell company, one of their managers, my company would like to thank you for your dramatic rescue of our employees, how did you learn those efforts you displayed", giving him the same answer he had given Walter before, the white man took the extended hand, shaking it in acknowledgement.

As the Shell man turned away, he asked, "is there any thing we could do for you", the white man accompanied him to his launch, both men stepped onto the launch, when it reached the platform, the whiter man lead the Shell manager onto the walkways between each station, indicating the double gate, between the two companies, he indicated they only had the keys for their gate, but had no key for both gates, so could never arrange any link up between both parties.

Then turning towards the ground flare stack, the white man indicate to the three black impressions on the surface of the six inch bund area around the flare stack, peering hard at what the white was indicating, the Shell manager asked "what are those black marks", before the white man answered, he stared directly into the Shell managers eyes, "bodies, burnt and blasted bodies", with his face blanched white, he asked "how", the white man stated, "locals who live in the swamps, having no power or any thing to light their lives, come to the flare stack, to scoop up any hydrocarbon liquid they can find, only no one knows when the flare stack will flare, consequently they are caught out and burnt to death, before being incinerated, as you can see, "why do they do it", asked the Shell manger, "because" said the white man, "they have nothing, yours and our companies never give or do any thing for them, so they steal five litre of condensate, "so we burn them", also, added the white man, indicating his platform and pipelines, "we also flare through the same system", the tragic look on the Shell managers face, began to crumble, "how can we stop this from happening" he asked.

Indicating to the flare the white man said, "this is a ground flare system, any thing that gets within 30 feet of that flare will be burnt and incinerated within seconds", again indicating to the flare, he simply stated, "we raise the flare to thirty or forty feet, so any one underneath, will feel the heat, but will not get burnt". "There is no way we can stop them from taking condensate liquid, what use is it to us". "I will have this changed a soon as possible" said the Shell manager, shaking hands, they parted, the Shell manager flew off in his helicopter, the white man returned to his platform.

PHILOMENA & BARRY

The arrival of the launch to the Jones Creek platform, presented the white man, with apprehension, because it was not one of the usual normal people who visited the white man. John Jones was basically the last person the white man expected to see, this far into the swamps, he was the manager of another company who oversaw all activities for the main clients, The Nigerian Petroleum Company, he related the following story to the white man.

One of his employees Barry Firman, who was known to the white man, had begun a relationship with a Nigerian business woman, between them they had decided, when he had finalized his divorced, with his estranged wife, with whom he had been battling for more than three years, they would get married, Barry would then arrange for her to come to England, obtaining visa's for her and her four year old son, having now been associated with with her for over two years, their feelings for each other had become an obsession, which related into an aggressive frame of mind, as his wife in England, would approach his employers offices demanding they pay her all of his previously earnest salary, which they did on repeatedly demanding overtures, leaving Barry usually very hard up.

Because of his association with Philomena, these problems did not cause Barry to much distress, as Philomena would fund Barry throughout these times, therefore as each day and month proceeded, they became even closer together. As Sara's demise had happened only weeks previously, Barry had arranged to return to England, with the view of halting his present wife, from badgering his company, into passing over his earned salary, to do so he had agreed to take three weeks off in England to resolve this particular issue.

Ten days after his departure, Philomena, travelling back from Port Harcourt, in eastern Nigeria, where she had been organizing her business, along one of the few roads that past through the jungle swamp regions, caught up with the never ending trail of large transport trucks, who always created huge dust clouds, as the totally unmade up roads were inch's deep in red dust, being behind these trucks was akin to driving in dense fog, she had seen on a bend a clearer section of roadway, ahead of the truck she was following, she therefore pulled out to over take the truck, a truck she had not seen, coming in the opposite direction met her half way up the truck she was overtaking, plowing into her car, killing both her and her son instantly, the driver of the truck she had tried to overtake, had not seen or noticed any thing, until the dust thinned and he could see the carnage behind his truck.

Obvious there was nothing anyone could do, traffic was routed around the crash site, as the local police gathered information regarding to the crash, they in their time acknowledged it was an accident, finding in her personal baggage, details of he relationship with Barry Firman, therefore they informed his employment company of this tragic accident, consequently as Barry was still away on his scheduled leave period, he was not informed, his return a week later was also met with a complete denial of information being given to him.

Finally when he was informed, his life was devastated, he blame every one for not letting him know, blaming every one for failing to contact him in England, but mostly he blamed his company for allowing him to be away. Sorrow and sadness took over, resulting in him trying to blot the events of by seriously drinking, local Nigerian operators, then began to invite him to further blot out the horrific accident, by pushing him to local prepared drugs, soon he became reliant on both the drugs and drink, this John Jones told the white man was the present problem, having completed his story to the white man, John Jones waited for the white man to reply, staring at John Jones, he asked "why me", John Jones with a tight grimace smile on his face, simply said "because I know you will fix it", continuing to look at John Jones, the white man shrugged his shoulders, "no promises, my way, do not ask, if I can get it sorted", John Jones held out his hand, "agreed", immediately descending the walk way to his launch, waving as he sailed away.

Two further days later, after returning from the swamp areas, to Warri, the white man had his driver pass by the compound where his rooms were located, for a clothing change, before driving him to the local restaurant he always used, Aunties Kitchen, across the other side of Warri, this however meant passing through the biggest bottleneck in Warri, the famed no way through, cross roads, every one between 16.00hrs and 20.30hrs would try to navigate this particular cross roads, usually ending up with a monstrous amounts of crashes and constant pile ups.

As they, the car driver and the white man approached the junction, his driver Saturday, told the white man to lock his door, spreading his hands, the white man asked "why" pointing Saturday, shouted "gunman", immediately the white man opened the door, stepped out, reached over and took the gun out of the robbers hand, instantly recognizing the robber as one of his pipeline workers, unloading the gun and stripping it down, before throwing it under other cars and trucks, then pushing his face into the robbers, said casually, "do not expect your drinking money this week, for this escapade", then reaching into his wallet, took out a twenty Nira note, gave it to the robber saying, "go and have a drink", the robber ran off, turning to the stall holder, asked her if the robber had taken any thing, the answer was no, so he gave her twenty Nita, for her troubles.

Finally passing the cross road junction, Saturday dropped the white man off at Aunties Kitchen, Charity {she was the owner, married to a Scotsman, who had originally started the restaurant}, greeted the white man, with a huge hug, "back again" she said, nodding his head he agreed with her, sitting at the bar she continued to talk to the white man, the door burst open, five men entered, four were local Nigerians the fifth was Barry Firman, there was much laughing and general horse play, until the white man turned around.

Suddenly the air became tense as he stood up, making his way towards Barry and his cohorts, immediately the white man clapped his hands over Barry's ears, the bar room was now deathly quiet, almost as a whisper, the white said to Barry, "come on Barry its me", as he local friends made a move forwards, the white pointed at two of them, "you two move out, or tomorrow there will be no work", backing off the four locals moved away, again the white man clapped his hands around Barrys ears, Barry was now totally red in his Face, still the white man did not move away, only getting closer, quick as a flash again, Barrys ears were clapped, this time Barry looked up, the white man finally spoke to him "at last" said the white man, "I now have your undivided attention, what the F'ing hell do you think you are doing, Philomena is dead, for that I'm sorry, but that is all the symphony you will get from me, do you wish for this to continue", "if not make your wishes known", Barry shock his head.

Still without moving away, the white man moved his hand up, Barry covered his ears, "O.K" said the white man "tomorrow you will book onto a plane, you will go back to England, you will finalize your banking details that you never completed, you will find a solicitor, you will finalize your divorce, then and only then you will return back to your employment company here in Nigeria, need I remind you, you now have a child to look after, are we clear on all of this", Barry nodded his head. "Should you fail to adhere to these suggestions, I will personally have Micheal and Graham, take you out into the swamp and loss you, now do you get it". For the first time since he arrived Barry spoke, "Yes", putting down his drink, Barry walked out of the bar room.

The next day there was a gentle bump at the landing stage to the platform, arriving at the top of the stairs as the other person also arrived, it was John Jones, smiling broadly, "what the hell did you say to him", he asked the white man, "why" said the white man, "he's on the plane to England" said John Jones, "is'nt that what you wanted" asked he white man, "I also told you not ask how or why, the matter is now closed, he will be back, but as the old Barry", "thank you for whatever you did", John Jones shook the white mans hand before leaving.

ACKNOWLEDGEMENT

At a lunch break later that week, a strange launch tied up at Jones Creeks short jetty, one of its crew dressed in coveralls, "some one here called the white man", he asked, acknowledging him the white man asked "why" handing a bottle, obviously of American whisky, to the white man, "this is from the captain of the rig platform, says sorry he could not slow down, but he had to be over a well by six, the next morning, would he the white man, accept this bottle as a thanks for his help. Calling Sid the bush bar owner over, he asked him to nail five bottle tops to a soft piece of wood, then wrap it up plastic, this Sid did, taking his pen, he wrote, "thank you, for your help and understanding, but it was fun", slipping the note under the plastic, he gave it to the rig worker, asking him to make sure the captain received it. Weeks later, the white man was informed, the American captain of the rig platform, had accepted the five stars, the white man had pinned to the piece of wood, it was now displayed at the front of the wheel house, Every time he looked at the American cracked out laughing

The Chinese whispers never stopped, all of Warri knew about the stripping down of Barry Firman. The bush telegraph became even louder, but then came FRAU GERTRUDE SHMITT.

FRAU GERTRUDE SHMITT

The bumping of a launch against the landing section at the bottom of the gangway, had alerted the white man to possible visitors, foot steps, soon followed, but not the usual booted sound steps, lighter more delicate timid steps, the white mans door opened, revealing Frau Shmitt, as she entered his office, she turned and locked the door, walking over to the white mans desk, hooking up one leg, she balanced her self, on the edge of the desk, carefully pulling and stretching the bottom of her dress skirt, without dropping his gaze the white man, held her gaze, asking to what do I have the pleasure of, by your unusual visit, moving his hands each side of his body, continuing to stare into Frau Shmitt's eyes, replying she stated I have heard about your association with the locals and the community as a whole, your other exploits have also not gone unnoticed, my question now is how long have you been on site in the swamp area's, placing her fingers to her lips, 5 and a half months I believe she stated, in all this time you have not taken any rest or days off, correct, she finished. Still maintaining his steady gaze, the white man inclined his head, that would be absolutely true he answered, my question is why does a director of the company, want to know how long I work for, smiling, still without moving her legs, she informed him, should he be ready or when he had decided to come out of the swamp area's, her villa had a vacant bedroom available, she would also have her regular chef, prepare a meal which she would be available at, again inclining his head whilst rising, the white man held the door open as Frau Shmitt departed.

PAYMENT SHORTAGE

The day had come for the company to hand over the compensation money to the young girl, aboard the Makaraba platform, by Paul Stricker, the naval guards swamp launch had picked up Stricker from the Odidi platform early in the morning, proceeded onwards towards the Jones Creek platform, the white man had by the companies head office management been nominated as the authority, to ensure that their directions had been adhered too, with correct procedures carried out. The naval guards had whilst they were en-route from Odidi to Jones Creek, placed the loaded money belt, that had been placed inside a strong companies envelope, inside a small recess on the small launch, idly the naval commander had picked up the envelope, hanging between his fingers, he stared at Paul Stricker, opening the envelope the naval commander began to count the money notes that were in the money belt, suddenly he shouted at Paul Stricker, money missing, money missing, Paul Stricker immediately began to also check count the money notes, screaming at the naval commander, there is only 88500 Nira, the naval guards on the launch turned their guns towards Paul Stricker, releasing the guns safety catches, Stricker waved his hands about, indicating it was not him that had reduced the money, they must have got in wrong in Warri.

Whilst the naval commander and Stricker continued to argue, which was slowly getting out of hand, with the other guards trying to hold Stricker, so he could be searched, the launch was rocked violently from side to side, nearly tipping over, whilst still cruising towards Jones Creek, finally the platform at Jones Creek came into view, Stricker broke free as the gangway appeared, leaping the six feet onto the landing platform, before running to the gangway onto the steps up to the offices, tripping on the bottom step, as the naval guard grabbed his foot, tipping Stricker onto the steps, placing his face inches from the poisonous snake that had been there, screaming Stricker leap up again jumping over the snake, bounding up the rest of the steps, making it into the white mans office, screaming shut the door.

RECOVERED PAYMENT FUNDS

The white man rose from his desk, pushed the lock pin down on the door, thereby stopping anyone from opening it any further, the enraged naval guards outside, pushed one of the rifles through the slightly open space, pulling the trigger, the bullet zipped around the office, as the white man grabbed Stricker, dragging him into the store room, before shutting and locking the store room door, then opening the main office door, confronting the naval commander, demanding to know what the problem was, whilst moving the naval commander and the two guards out of the office. The naval commander and the white man moved to a totally quiet area, where the naval commander informed the white man of the events that had happened, since they had left Odidi, taking the naval commander back into the main office area, the white man and the naval commander, again counted out the money from the money belt, both agreed there was only 88500 Nira.

Locking the naval commander outside of the office, the white man returned to the store room, confronting Stricker with the evidence of 88500 Nina being missing, Stricker stated that was all he had been given, the blow from the white man landing straight in Stricker soft stomach, rendering him breathless, demanding to know what he had done with the rest of the money, Stricker pointing down at his waist, the white man noticed another money belt, raising his fist again at Stricker, the money belt was removed, locking him back into the store room, the white man opened the door to the naval commander, indicating the other money belt, they both counted out the money again, 177000 Nira, placing both money belts into the envelope, the white man sealed the envelope, signed the fastening tag, before presenting it to the naval commander.

FINAL PAYMENT TO THE MAKARABA FAMILY

Finally with the naval guards and Paul Stricker, who through out the last section of the trip, was handcuffed to one of the naval guards, continued its journey onwards to Makaraba, upon arrival at the companies platform, all participants were gathered onto the accommodation section of the rig, through the resident engineer, first the village chief was thanked for his part in the wrangling for the compensation money, the money totals were counted by Paul Stricker, who grimaced as he handed over 25000 Nira to the village chief, verifying the balance of 152000 Nira, Paul Stricker, although looking visually sick, handed this money sum to the young girls parents, who immediately handed the total money sum over to the village chief, requesting that he should hold it for the parents, until they would need it, written documents were made out, every one then signed or made their mark, a set of document papers were handed to the village chief, whilst the companies chief engineer kept the original signed papers, Paul Strickers face was blanched white, as he was transported back to the white man's platform, at Jones Creek.

Upon the arrival of the navy commanders launch, Paul Stricker was dropped off, the naval commander and crew, continued on their way to Warri, Paul Stricker was met by the white man, who checked the offered envelope, for the correct signatures, satisfied the white man lead Paul Stricker into his office, requesting to know why he had tried to rob the company and injured family, with no response from Paul Stricker, the white man set out a set of rules, explaining to him, provided he kept up the requirements dictated by the white man, nothing would be broadcast to the management in Warri, Paul

Stricker immediately agreed, the white man reminded him should he not keep his end of the agreement, this incident would be directly reported. Acknowledging this was given by the nod of his head, thereafter the white man, called his launch bosun to deposit Paul Stricker back to his base platform at Odidi.

Two days later, Walter, the project managing director, arrived at Jones Creek, greeting the white man he shook his hand, before saying "thank you for your handling of the problem", the white man stared at Walter, before saying "what problem", both men then laughed, "I will deal with Paul" Walter stated, the white man, shook his head, "no" he said, "leave every thing as it is ", Walter agreed.

ESCAPED PRISONERS DESPARATE ACTION

Since his escape from the law courts in Lagos, the prisoner had begun to make his way back towards the area and location, near to where he had previously been living, when he was arrested, to avoid the police, he had made his way along the beach, sometimes close to the road, some times far enough for him to feel safe, it was very slow going, each day as he moved along local fishermen would shout at him, asking him to give them a hand, he always agreed, not wanting to stand out, this then resulted in him spending more than one day with different groups of fishermen, as his work ethics increased, his travel time slowed again, consequently it took him over three months to traverse from Lagos to the swamp area near Warri.

Finally he recognized the area he had arrived in, remembering all the beatings he had suffered when he was caught at Makaraba, made him direct all his efforts into his soon return, avoiding streets where he was known, he found a room so he could rest before setting out on the last leg of his return.

Early the following morning, before most people were about, he made his way to the boat yard, hundreds of boats both large and small bobbed up and down in the placid water, towards the outer limits of the boats, canoes were tied, selecting one, unfastening the mooring rope, he paddled away, just as he was to disappear around the exit from the boat yard, a load shout made him turn his head, the canoe owner had arrived jus as he set off, recognizing this man he dug the paddle deeper into the water, swiftly rounding the corner and disappearing.

Having avoided the risk of being caught in the boat yard, swiftly he paddled out into the main creek system, mangrove trees and their vegetation hung over dipping into the creeks swamp water, paddling close to these area's, he made it to the main channel swamp creek, knowing this would lead him into the Jones Creek, from which the Makaraba creek forked off, continuing to paddle at a rate he could maintain, for he knew there was more than 10 miles to go. The faint sound of an engine sent him immediately into the over hung vegetation, without moving he watched as the naval guards launch motored slowly past, before circling, passing closer to where he was hiding, scanning the trees and growths the naval launch stopped its engine, drifting with the incoming tidal water, it passed 30 feet from his hiding place, observing no movement or any sudden tree movement, the naval launch commander signaled for the launch to move on.

The escaped prisoner now knew that the naval guards launch, with the naval guards and police, were between him and the Makaraba creek, slowly whilst still under the branch's hang overs, the escaped prisoner paddle back down the creek, before branching off into a smaller twist creek system, as he had spent most of his growing years in and around these area's, he also knew that these smaller creeks often were the homes of the largest crocodiles, his crushing desire to take revenge on the people who had captured him, also against the villagers for assisting in his arrest, had become his over all forced focus that was driving him, framing in his mind what he would do when he arrived at Makaraba, as the village chief had wanted to castrate him then behead him, he would return the favour, by castrating him first whilst he was still alive, then behead him, before he died.

The tributary creek was long and twisted, circulating endless miles to his journey, as he paddled his canoe through the twisted branch#s of the mangrove trees, he avoided over hanging contrails of growth, not knowing if they were snakes or not. Finally he reached the exit from the small creek into the main swamp water flowing system.

His arrival at this point, made him hid again in the over hanging vegetation, as the naval guards launch slowly passed this creek exit, unseen by the escaped prisoner, the naval launch had dropped one of the guards into a larger mangrove tree, just above the swamp water level, he was only about 25 feet away from the escaped prisoner, already he was lining up his rifle for a shot, whilst the naval launch had continued to cruise along the swamp banks, still looking for the prisoner, laying over the trees branch's whilst taking aim. The escaped prisoner, had paddled his canoe out of the small creek, the launch's engine sound had faded away, he started to move further out of the small creek.

Suddenly there was movement behind the escaped prisoner canoe, an enormous crocodiles head broke the surface of the water, the naval guard who was perfectly in line as the crocodiles head raised above the swamp water, pulled his trigger, remembering what his training instructor had always screamed at him, aim for the eye's, aim for the eye's, the rifle kicked in his hands, but the bullet, went straight into the center of the fully open crocodiles eye, passing directly into its brain, causing the crocodile to rear up. Having heard the shot being fired, the escaped prisoner had begun to stand up in the small canoe, twisting as he did so, the huge crocodile in its surge movement after being shot was now almost over the top of him, crashing down in its death throws, the crocodile collapsed back into the swamp water, crushing the canoe and the escaped prisoner, still in its death throws, the crocodile had through its agony, opened its extremely large jaws, whilst the escaped prisoner floundering to regain the surface was moving away from the dyeing beast, as the crocodile snapped its jaws back together, they caught the prisoners inner thighs, along with the lower sections of his buttocks, also snared were his sexual organs, even though it was in its death throws, it began to twist, gurgling swamp water the prisoner screams erupted as his head broke the surface, with each movement of the twisting crocodile, the prisoner was dragged back under water, although his screams were bellowed at his full lung strength, nothing was heard, for as each scream made his gasp for air, he drowned.

Lesser crocodiles who had been sunning their selves on muddy banks, were sliding into the swamp waters, swimming towards the ongoing water thrashing created by the now nearly dead enormous crocodile final killing rolls, they to began joining in the melee that was ensuing, clamping their jaws onto sections of flesh the floated to the surface, as the enormous crocodile continued its death roll, suddenly it stopped, sections of the prisoners body floated to the surface, eagerly gobbled up by the ever increasing number of lesser crocodiles gathering.

The naval guards launch had returned towards where they had dropped off the first naval guard, observing the melee of crocodiles who had drifted with the incoming tidal flow, half a mile into the swamp area, from his tree branch position, the first guard dropped into the launch, immediately the coxswain boosted the engines away from the still entangled melee of crocodiles. Leaning over the side, the first guard vomited whilst he moaned trying to relate what he had seen, shaking and vomiting he slowly informed the others guards and policeman the result of shooting the crocodile through its eye, the guard commander took a note book out of his uniform breast pocket, opened it at the page where the prisoner details were written, circling this notation and drawing two lines under it he wrote, now dead.

Although the escaped rapist prisoners life had now been terminated by the enormous crocodile, only the naval guards and the policeman, would actually know how it had finished, never would they realize or even know this had been Sara's dyeing wish, cursing the Nigerian rapist for his terrifying horrific sexual violation of the young Makaraba girl, whilst she felt extremely deep sorrow for the companies employee who had been taken by another crocodile. Nor would anyone ever know that the crocodile that had taken the escaped prisoner, had been the same crocodile that had finally ended Sara's life.

Police would later recover debris from the swamp area banks, before interring the findings into a shallow crave with one word on the wooden cross, RAPIST, Sara's body was never recovered, no one ever reported her death, there never would be a grave with a name and markings, just the five bottle tops, nailed onto a swamp mangrove tree root, with the beer bottles company symbol showing, stars, five in total, on the instructions of the white man.

THE WHITE MAN

Gradually as time and days moved on, the white man became involved in most working projects, that effected every one of the companies distant located platforms, organizing the final completion to hand over of commissioned plants, having been personally involved in all of the sequenced events mentioned in this second book of "African Jungle Women, Ling life.--Just living", Book 2. The white man elected to travel to and visit Warri, calling from Jones Creek he contacted the companies head office, in Warri, declaring he would be travelling, Walter the project manager, replied, "my boat, leaving now" "thank you" from Jones Creek, "villa 14" stated a co-worker, "thank you" again from Jones Creek, a soft woman voice cut in these communications, stating, "my driver will pick you up, at the boat yard", "villa 6" will be ready. There was no reply, the radio communication had shut down. On the white mans arrival at the boat yard later that night, a driver drove him directly to "villa 14", 6 months of constant jungle living was resolved with an extremely pleasant evening meal followed by a large portion of deep sleep.

FAU GERTRUDE SCHMITT

The white mans visit to the companies main office had been to met and discuss with the management team, problems that had been found and resolved on site, through out the swamp production platforms, as part of the directorship of the oil companies management team, she was deeply involved, as she was the coordinator of the complete project. Whilst these involved discussions were ensured, she totally ignored all members of the team, specifically the white man.

A WOMEN SCORNED
STYLED
BY FRAU GERTRUDE SCHMITT

On completion of his discussions and companies head office visit, the white man returned to the swamp jungle living quarters, continuing with his companies duties, repeatedly making daily numerous launch journey's throughout the swamp area's, his arrival back at the location of his housing coincided with a letter issued from Warri, directing that the white man's contract with the oil company was to terminate on 20th September, signed by Frau Schmitt.. Referring this letter to the Nigerian National Oil Company head office, they in turn held discussions with the construction oil company, stating that this letter could not be issued, Frau Gertrude Schmitt had after issuing the letter, returned to the companies main head offices back in Germany, again she refused to halt or rescind the action and termination, of the white man, this was followed by two days of Nigerian National oil company discussions over this problem, resulting in the construction oil company being given a month to wind up their present area's of construction, before vacating their overall contract to the project.

The following day after the white mans departure from the contracting oil companies project, 21st September, the Nigerian National oil company, instructed the contracting oil company, to totally cease all its works, every where throughout this project, instructing them to leave and vacate Nigeria as soon as possible, within one day, furnishing the construction oil company with valid exit flight tickets, they would then have six months to remove all there equipment from Nigeria.

ABOUT THE AUTHOR

Since his childhood, the author has taken part in numerous facets of life, volunteering for the merchant navy, sailing throughout the Middle east, India, Singapore and other far eastern countries, also including the complete southern sections of Australia, before he attained the the living age of eighteen, before volunteering into the R.A.F as a marine radio operator on air sea rescue bases, which is where he became involved in the military, as the first British troupes to be directly posted to Cyprus, before and throughout the Suez crisis emergency mid 1956, receiving an active service medal for this engagement. After these episodes he spent 2 years in chemical rubber industry, followed by a long spell, 9 years in the compound fertilizers manufacturing industry, before entering into the oil and gas industries, before taking on the life of the expat overseas oil and gas worker, spending the next 43 years travelling the world whilst expanding his greater knowledge, throughout these times became totally competent within this industry, to the extent of resolving production problems and numerous dangerous happenings, specifically dealing with a 500,000bbl floating roof tank fire on the Bahamas Oil Refinery complex, successfully extinguishing the flames, whilst protecting the local village population houses and homes, that were within the fire and flame area of the blazing tank, without any loss of production, or reduction of production rates.

www.ingramcontent.com/pod-product-compliance
Lightning Source LLC
LaVergne TN
LVHW041536060526
838200LV00037B/1004

With the news of this contract loss, the German main office company directors, held an emergency meeting, relating to this present situation, forming another company with a close rival, they renamed their previous company under the rules previously set out.

FRAU GERTRUDE SCHMITT was invited to the new companies head office, the one she had always attended, the new managing director read out the previously prepared statement, to her, in which it was clearly stated that she was no longer a director of the company, as it had been reformed and her membership on the board was not longer required, a look of horror filled her face, her face went crimson with rage, she stammered "you can not do this", screaming she jumped to her feet, pacing up and down, whilst still shouting at the director, until finally she flopped back into her chair, "why" she shouted, "why" again she asked, the new director shrugged his shoulders, simple he said, because of THE WHITE MAN.

Had Sara survived throughout her absolutely tragic life, the white man hoped she would have felt some joy knowing that the child abuser had paid for his crimes, that the enormous crocodile had too been destroyed, little could have been done about the companies drowned engineer, apart from them accepting compensation. But he hoped she would acknowledge the white mans refusal to dine individually with Frau Schmitt.

Maybe, not quite finished

ABOUT THIS SPECIFIC BOOK

Harking back to the first book, "African Jungle Women Living Life -- Just Living" reminded me of the base main reason for the first book, we, people of the "rest" of the world, live our life on the justified prognosis, that we have been and were conceived and born into a worldly life system, that nurtures and sustains the vast majority of whatever peoples, that have become residents of those countries, who make up the complete worldly nations of this world, through and because of these systems, that are the simple fact and truths, all and every lives from their original first breath, throughout their growing years, followed by the infancy years, until achieving teen age adulthood, with all its tantrum, upheavals, aligned with unmitigated demands, coupled with bizarre behaviour patterns, and constant impossible requests, into the flamboyant people they aspire too, mostly due to the area and locations, then the world allows them to reside and live in, because of the flamboyancy of the world.

However, there are segments of peoples, coupled with sections of the greater worlds population, who simply by location, area and the simplest of reasons, birth, along with no flamboyancy, will never be given, receive or simply are granted any of the previous indicated life's normal balanced ways, or the reasons for their lives being lived, within these particular devastating normally uninhabitable worldly area locations, which in simple terms, commits them to function throughout their entire lives, in or at locations that take away every single choice of a life, that is given so freely by birth.

Thereafter being at the mercy of every jungle elements, as they carry out their totally meagre lives, never are they considered for any form of location or area compensation, although their area's of living can be exploited, through the energy companies desire to enhance the populated worlds requirements, for power, transport, along with their constant need to provide a more secure lives for the greater populations.

They function in these area's from birth until death, never experiencing clear clean water supplies, have recourse to a normal flushing toilet systems, have electricity that has been supplied by a power grid system, therefore living their lives in a constant semi darkness, that is only deepened by the passing of natural day light, when their normal lives go into shut down, until the morning sun rises again. Should they suffer from any normal life illnesses, they are never offered or receive any local or social medical treatment, simply how can they, their homes, their points of residence are within the unremitting bonds of the swamps.